B.C

D1264096

Wisdom for Modern Man

Proverbs and Ecclesiastes
from
THE OLD TESTAMENT
in Today's English Version

AMERICAN BIBLE SOCIETY
New York

PROVERBS AND ECCLESIASTES
in Today's English Version

This portion of Holy Scripture in Today's English Version is a part of the Old Testament of the Bible. We urge you next to read the entire New Testament, which may be secured from your church, religious bookstore, or the American Bible Society.

Printed in U.S.A.

Eng. Portions Proverbs and Ecclesiastes TEV460P
A.B.S.-1973-250,000-750,000-CL-3   © American Bible Society, 1972

PREFACE

THE BIBLE CONTAINS many types of writing, which arose
out of different situations and which speak to people in
different situations. No books of Scripture are more down-
to-earth in their recognition of our practical, everyday
concerns than those which are called "Wisdom Liter-
ature." *Proverbs* and *Ecclesiastes* are two of those books.

The subject matter of *Proverbs* teaches that religion is
concerned with the common problems of living. The book
begins with the reminder that "to have knowledge, you
must fear God," but goes on to deal with matters not only
of religious morality, but also of common sense and good
manners. Its many short sayings reveal the insights of the
ancient Israelite teachers about what a wise man will do in
certain situations. Some of these concern family relations,
others business dealings. Some deal with matters of eti-
quette in social relationships, and others with the need for
self-control. The proverbs have much to say about such
qualities as humility, patience, respect for the poor, and
loyalty to friends.

The short book of *Ecclesiastes* contains the thoughts of
a man, perhaps an old man, concerned with the shortness
of life. He wonders if it has all been worthwhile, and many
of his thoughts appear negative and even depressing. But
all people, if they are honest, think this way at times, and
the very fact that *Ecclesiastes* is in the Bible teaches that
the faith of the Bible is broad enough to find room for
such relentless self-honesty. Many have taken comfort in
seeing themselves in the mirror of *Ecclesiastes,* and have
discovered that the same Bible that reflects these thoughts
also offers the hope that gives life its greatest meaning.

Like the New Testament in *Today's English Version,* this
is a distinctively new translation that does not conform to
traditional vocabulary and style. It seeks to express the
meaning of the Hebrew text in words and forms accepted
as standard by people everywhere who employ English as
a means of communication.

Where there is general agreement that the Hebrew text
cannot be translated as it now stands, the translation
employs the evidence of other ancient texts or follows
present-day scholarly consensus. All such modifications
are identified in footnotes.

v

They're always ready to kill

PROVERBS

The Value of Proverbs

1 The proverbs of Solomon, son of David and king of Israel.

² Here are proverbs that will help you recognize wisdom and good advice, and understand sayings with deep meaning. ³ They can teach you how to live intelligently, and how to be honest, just, and fair. ⁴ They can make an inexperienced person clever, and teach young men how to be resourceful. ⁵ These proverbs can even add to the knowledge of wise men, and give guidance to the educated, ⁶ so that they can understand the hidden meanings of proverbs, and the problems that wise men raise.

Advice to Young Men

⁷ To have knowledge, you must first fear the Lord. Stupid people have no respect for wisdom, and refuse to learn.

⁸ Son, listen to what your father teaches you, and pay attention to what your mother says. ⁹ Their teaching will improve your character as a handsome turban or a necklace helps your appearance.

¹⁰ Son, when sinners tempt you, don't give in. ¹¹ Suppose they say, "Come on; let's find someone and kill him! Let's attack innocent people for the fun of it! ¹² They may be alive and well when we find them, but they'll be dead when we're through with them! ¹³ We'll find all kinds of riches, and fill our houses with loot! ¹⁴ Come join us, and we'll all share what we steal."

¹⁵ Son, don't go with people like that. Stay away from them. ¹⁶ They can't wait to do something bad. They're always ready to kill. ¹⁷ It does no good to spread a net when the bird you want to catch is watching, ¹⁸ but men like that are setting a trap for themselves, a trap in which they will die. ¹⁹ Robbery always claims the life of the robber—this is what happens to[a] anyone who lives by stealing.

---

[a] *One ancient translation* what happens to; *Hebrew* the path of.

Wisdom Calls

[20] Listen! Wisdom is calling out in the streets and market-places, [21] calling loudly at the city gates, and anywhere else that people come together:

[22] "Foolish people! How long do you want to be foolish? How long will you enjoy making fun of knowledge? Will you never learn? [23] Listen when I reprimand you; I will give you good advice and share my knowledge with you. [24] I have been calling you, inviting you to come, but you would not listen. You paid no attention to me. [25] You have ignored all my advice, and have not been willing for me to correct you. [26] So, when you get into trouble, I will laugh at you. I will make fun of you when terror strikes—[27] when it comes on you like a storm, bringing fierce winds of trouble, and you are in pain and misery. [28] Then you will call for wisdom, but I will not answer. You may look for me everywhere, but you will not find me. [29] You have never had any use for knowledge, and have always refused to fear the Lord. [30] You have never wanted my advice or paid any attention when I corrected you. [31] So then, you will get what you deserve, and your own actions will make you sick. [32] Inexperienced people die because they reject wisdom. Stupid people are destroyed by their own lack of concern. [33] But whoever listens to me will have security. He will be safe, with no reason to be afraid."

The Rewards of Wisdom

2 Son, learn what I teach you, and never forget what I tell you to do. [2] Listen to what is wise, and try to understand it. [3] Yes, beg for knowledge; plead for insight. [4] Look for it as hard as you would for silver, or some hidden treasure. [5] If you do, you will know what it means to fear the Lord, and you will succeed in learning about God. [6] It is the Lord who gives wisdom. Knowledge and understanding come from him. [7] He provides help and protection for righteous, honest men. [8] He protects those who treat others fairly, and guards those who are devoted to him.

[9] If you listen to me you will know what is right, just, and fair. You will know what you should do. [10] You will become wise, and your knowledge will give you pleasure. [11] Your insight and understanding will protect you, [12] and

prevent you from doing the wrong thing. They will keep you away from people who stir up trouble by what they say—[13] men who have abandoned a righteous life to live in the darkness of sin, [14] men who find pleasure in doing wrong and enjoy senseless evil, [15] undependable men who cannot be trusted.

[16] You will be able to resist any immoral woman who tries to seduce you with her smooth talk, [17] who is faithless to her own husband, and forgets her sacred vows. [18] If you go to her house you are traveling the road to death. To go there is to approach the land of the dead.[b] [19] No one who visits her ever comes back. He never returns to the road to life. [20] So you must follow the example of good men, and live a righteous life. [21] Righteous men—men of integrity—will live in this land of ours. [22] But God will snatch wicked men from the land, and pull sinners out of it like plants from the ground.

Advice to Young Men

3 Son, don't forget what I teach you. Always remember what I tell you to do. [2] My teaching will give you a long and prosperous life. [3] Never let go of loyalty and faithfulness. Tie them around your neck; write them on your heart. [4] If you do this, both God and men will be pleased with you.

[5] Trust in the Lord with all your heart. Never rely on what you think you know. [6] Remember the Lord in everything you do, and he will show you the right way. [7] Never let yourself think that you are wiser than you are; simply fear the Lord, and refuse to do wrong. [8] If you do, it will be like good medicine, healing your wounds and easing your pains. [9] Honor the Lord by making him an offering from the best of all that your land produces. [10] If you do, your barns will be filled with grain. You will have so much wine that you won't be able to store it all.

[11] Son, when the Lord corrects you, pay close attention and take it as a warning. [12] The Lord corrects those he loves, as a father corrects a son of whom he is proud. [13] Happy is the man who becomes wise—who comes to have understanding. [14] There is more profit in it than there

---

[b] LAND OF THE DEAD: It was thought that the dead continued to exist in a dark world under the ground.

is in silver; it is worth more to you than gold. ¹⁵ Wisdom is more valuable than jewels; nothing you could want can compare with it. ¹⁶ Wisdom offers you long life, as well as wealth and honor. ¹⁷ Wisdom can make your life pleasant, and lead you safely through it. ¹⁸ Those who become wise are happy; wisdom will give them life.

> ¹⁹ The Lord created the earth by his wisdom;
> he set the sky in place by his knowledge.
> ²⁰ His wisdom caused the rivers to flow,
> and the clouds to give rain to the earth.

²¹ Son, hold on to your wisdom and insight. Never let them get away from you. ²² They will provide you with life—a pleasant and happy life. ²³ You can go safely on your way and never so much as stumble. ²⁴ You will not be afraid when you go to bed, and you will sleep soundly through the night. ²⁵ You will not have to worry about sudden disasters, such as come on the wicked like a storm. ²⁶ The Lord will keep you safe. He will not let you fall into a trap.

²⁷ Do good to those who need it, whenever you possibly can. ²⁸ Never tell your neighbor to wait until tomorrow if you can help him now. ²⁹ Don't plan anything that will hurt your neighbor; he lives beside you, trusting you. ³⁰ Don't argue with someone for no reason, when he has never done you any harm. ³¹ Don't be jealous of violent people or decide to act as they do, ³² because the Lord hates people who do evil, but he takes righteous men into his confidence. ³³ The Lord puts a curse on the homes of wicked men, but blesses the homes of the righteous. ³⁴ He has no use for conceited people, but shows favor to those who are humble. ³⁵ Wise men will gain an honorable reputation, but stupid men will only add to their own disgrace.

The Benefits of Wisdom

4 Sons, listen to what your father teaches you. Pay attention, and you will have understanding. ² What I am teaching you is good, so remember it all. ³ When I was only a little boy, my parents' only son, ⁴ my father would teach me. He would say, "Remember what I say and never forget it. Do as I tell you, and you will live. ⁵ Get wisdom and insight! Do not forget or ignore what I say. ⁶ Do not abandon wisdom, and she will protect you; love her, and

she will keep you safe. ⁷ Getting wisdom is the wisest thing you can do. Whatever else you get, get insight. ⁸ Love wisdom, and she will make you great. Embrace her, and she will bring you honor. ⁹ She will be your crowning glory."

¹⁰ Listen to me, son. Take seriously what I am telling you and you will live a long life. ¹¹ I have taught you wisdom and the right way to live. ¹² Nothing will stand in your way if you walk wisely, and you will not stumble when you run. ¹³ Always remember what you have learned. Your education is your life—guard it well. ¹⁴ Do not go where evil men go. Do not follow the example of the wicked. ¹⁵ Don't do it! Keep away from evil! Refuse it, and go on your way. ¹⁶ Wicked people cannot sleep unless they have done something wrong. They lie awake unless they have hurt someone. ¹⁷ Wickedness and violence are like food and drink to them.

¹⁸ The road the righteous travel is like the sunrise, getting brighter and brighter until daylight has come. ¹⁹ The road of the wicked, however, is dark as night. They fall, but cannot see what they have stumbled over.

²⁰ Son, pay attention to what I say. Listen to my words. ²¹ Never let them get away from you. Remember them, and love them. ²² They will give life and health to anyone who understands them. ²³ Be careful how you think; your life is shaped by your thoughts. ²⁴ Never say something that isn't true. Have nothing to do with lies and misleading words. ²⁵ Look straight ahead, with honest confidence; don't hang your head in shame. ²⁶ Be sure you know what you are doing, and whatever you do will turn out right. ²⁷ Avoid evil and walk straight ahead. Don't go one step off the right way.

Warning against Adultery

5 Son, pay attention, and listen to my wisdom and insight. ² Then you will know how to behave properly, and your words will show that you have knowledge. ³ The lips of another man's wife may be as sweet as honey and her kisses smooth as olive oil, ⁴ but when it is all over she leaves you nothing but bitterness and pain. ⁵ She will take you down to the land of the dead;^c the road she walks

^c LAND OF THE DEAD: See 2.18.

is the road to death. ⁶ She does not stay[d] on the road to life; she wanders off, but you are not aware of it.

⁷ Now listen to me, sons, and never forget what I am saying. ⁸ Keep away from such a woman! Don't even go near her door! ⁹ If you do, others will gain the respect that you once had, and you will die young at the hands of merciless men. ¹⁰ Yes, strangers will take all your wealth, and what you have worked for will belong to someone else. ¹¹ You will lie groaning on your deathbed, your flesh and muscles being eaten away, ¹² and you will say, "Why would I never learn? Why would I never let anyone correct me? ¹³ I wouldn't listen to my teachers. I paid no attention to them. ¹⁴ And suddenly I found myself publicly disgraced."

¹⁵ Be faithful to your own wife, and give your love to her alone. ¹⁶ Children that you have by other women will do you no good. ¹⁷ Your children should grow up to help you, not strangers. ¹⁸ So be happy with your wife and find your joy with the girl you married—¹⁹ pretty and graceful as a deer. Let her charms keep you happy; let her surround you with her love. ²⁰ Son, why should you give your love to another woman? Why should you prefer the charms of another man's wife? ²¹ The Lord sees everything you do. Wherever you go, he is watching. ²² The sins of a wicked man are a trap. He gets caught in the net of his own sin. ²³ He dies because he has no self-control. His utter stupidity will take him to his grave.

More Warnings

6 Son, have you promised to be responsible for someone else's debt? ² Have you been caught by your own words, trapped by your own promises? ³ Well then, son, you are in that man's power, but this is how to get out of it: hurry to him, and beg him to release you. ⁴ Don't let yourself go to sleep or even stop to rest. ⁵ Get out of the trap like a bird or a deer escaping a hunter.

⁶ Lazy people should learn a lesson from the way ants live. ⁷ They have no leader, chief, or ruler, ⁸ but they store up their food during the summer, getting ready for winter. ⁹ How long is the lazy man going to lie around? When is he ever going to get up? ¹⁰ "I'll just take a short nap," he

---

d *Some ancient translations* She does not stay; *Hebrew* Or else she will stay.

Your children should grow up to help you

says; "I'll fold my hands and rest a while." ¹¹ But while he sleeps, poverty will attack him like an armed robber.

¹² Worthless, wicked people go around telling lies. ¹³ They wink and make gestures to deceive you, ¹⁴ all the while planning evil in their perverted minds, stirring up trouble everywhere. ¹⁵ Because of this, disaster will strike them without warning, and they will be fatally wounded.

¹⁶⁻¹⁹ There are seven things that the Lord hates and cannot tolerate:

A proud look,
   a lying tongue,
      hands that kill innocent people,
         a mind that thinks up wicked plans,
            someone hurrying off to do evil,
               a witness who tells one lie after another,
                  and a man who stirs up trouble among friends.

Warning against Adultery

²⁰ Son, do what your father tells you and never forget what your mother taught you. ²¹ Keep their words with you always, locked in your heart. ²² Their teaching will lead you when you travel, protect you at night, and advise you during the day. ²³ Their instructions are a shining light; their correction can teach you how to live. ²⁴ It can keep you away from bad women, from the seductive words of other men's wives. ²⁵ Don't be tempted by their beauty; don't be trapped by their flirting eyes. ²⁶ A man can hire a prostitute for the price of a loaf of bread, but adultery will cost him all he has.

²⁷ Can you carry fire against your chest without burning your clothes? ²⁸ Can you walk on hot coals without burning your feet? ²⁹ It is just as dangerous to sleep with another man's wife. Whoever does it will suffer. ³⁰ People don't despise a thief if he steals food when he is hungry; ³¹ yet if he is caught, he must pay back seven times more— he must give up everything he has. ³² But a man who commits adultery doesn't have good sense. He is just destroying himself. ³³ He will be dishonored and beaten up —permanently disgraced. ³⁴ A husband is never angrier than when he is jealous; his revenge knows no limits. ³⁵ He will not accept any payment; no amount of gifts will satisfy his anger.

7 Son, remember what I say and never forget what I tell you to do. [2] Do what I say and you will live. Be as careful to follow my teaching as you are to protect your eyes. [3] Keep my teaching with you all the time; write it on your heart. [4] Treat wisdom as your sister, and insight as your closest friend. [5] They will keep you away from other men's wives, from women with seductive words.

The Immoral Woman

[6] Once I was looking out the window of my house, [7] and I saw many inexperienced young men, but noticed one foolish boy in particular. [8] He was walking along the street near the corner where a certain woman lived. He was passing near her house [9] in the evening, after it was dark. [10] And then she met him; she was dressed like a prostitute, and was making plans. [11] (She was bold and shameless, always walking the streets. [12] She would stand waiting at any corner, sometimes in the streets, sometimes in the marketplace.) [13] She threw her arms around the young man, kissed him, looked him straight in the eye, and said, [14] "I made my offerings today, and have the meat from the sacrifices. [15] So I came out looking for you. I wanted to find you, and here you are! [16] I've covered my bed with sheets of colored linen from Egypt. [17] I've perfumed it with myrrh, aloes, and cinnamon. [18] Come on. Let's make love all night long. We'll be happy in each other's arms. [19] My husband isn't at home. He's on a long trip. [20] He took plenty of money with him, and won't be back for two weeks." [21] So she tempted him with her charms, and he gave in to her smooth talk. [22] Suddenly he was going with her like an ox on the way to be slaughtered, like a deer prancing into a trap[e] [23] where an arrow would pierce its heart. He was like a bird going into a net—he did not know that his life was in danger.

[24] Now then, sons, listen to me. Pay attention to what I say. [25] Do not let such a woman win your heart; don't go wandering after her. [26] She has been the ruin of many men, and caused the death of too many to count. [27] Go to her house and you are on the way to the land of the dead.[f] It is a shortcut to death.

[e] like a deer prancing into a trap; Hebrew unclear.
[f] LAND OF THE DEAD: See 2.18.

In Praise of Wisdom

8 Listen! Wisdom is calling out.
    Reason is making herself heard.
2 On the hilltops near the road
    and at the crossroads she stands.
3 At the entrance to the city,
    beside the gates she calls:
4 "I appeal to you, mankind;
    I call to every man on earth.
5 Are you immature? Learn to be mature.
    Are you foolish? Learn to have sense.
6 Listen to my excellent words;
    all I tell you is right.
7 What I say is the truth;
    lies are hateful to me.
8 Everything I say is true;
    nothing is false or misleading.
9 To the man with insight, it is all clear;
    to the well-informed, it is all plain.
10 Choose my instruction instead of silver;
    choose knowledge rather than the finest gold.

11 I am Wisdom, I am better than jewels;
    nothing you want can compare with me.
12 I am Wisdom, and I have insight,
    I have knowledge and sound judgment.
13 To fear the Lord is to hate evil;
    I hate pride and arrogance,
    evil ways and false words.
14 I make plans and carry them out.
    I have understanding, and I am strong.
15 I help kings to rule
    and rulers to make good laws.
16 Every ruler on earth rules with my help,
    statesmen and noblemen alike.
17 I love those who love me;
    whoever looks for me can find me.
18 I have riches and honor to give,
    prosperity and success.
19 What you get from me is better than the
        finest gold,
    better than the purest silver.

²⁰ I walk the way of righteousness;
  I follow the paths of justice,
²¹ giving wealth to those who love me,
  filling their houses with treasures.

²² The Lord created me first of all,
  the first of his works, long ago.
²³ I was made in the very beginning,
  at the first, before the world began.
²⁴ I was born before the oceans,
  when there were no springs of water.
²⁵ I was born before the mountains,
  before the hills were set in place,
²⁶ before God made the earth and its fields,
  or even the first handful of soil.
²⁷ I was there when he set the sky in place,
  when he stretched the horizon across the
    ocean,
²⁸ when he placed the clouds in the sky,
  when he opened the springs of the ocean
²⁹ and ordered the waters of the sea
  to rise no further than he said.
  I was there when he laid the earth's foun-
    dations.
³⁰ I was beside him like an architect,
  I was his daily source of joy,
  always happy in his presence—
³¹ happy with the world
  and pleased with the human race.

³² Now, young men, listen to me.
  Do as I say and you will be happy.
³³ Listen to what you are taught.
  Be wise; do not neglect it.
³⁴ The man who listens to me will be happy—
  the man who stays at my door every day,
  waiting at the entrance to my home.
³⁵ The man who finds me finds life,
  and the Lord will be pleased with him.
³⁶ The man who does not find me hurts himself;
  anyone who hates me loves death."

Wisdom and Stupidity

9 Wisdom has built her house, and made seven columns for it. ² She has had an animal killed for a feast, mixed spices in the wine, and set the table. ³ She has sent her servant girls to call out from the highest place in town: ⁴ "Come in, ignorant people!" And to the foolish man she says, ⁵ "Come, eat my food and drink the wine that I have mixed. ⁶ Leave the company of ignorant people, and live. Follow the way of knowledge."

⁷ If you correct a conceited man, you will only be insulted. If you reprimand an evil man, you will only get hurt. ⁸ Never correct a conceited man; he will hate you for it. But if you correct a wise man, he will respect you. ⁹ Anything you say to a wise man will make him wiser. Whatever you tell a righteous man will add to his knowledge.

¹⁰ To be wise you must first fear the Lord. If you know the Holy One, you have understanding. ¹¹ Wisdom will add years to your life. ¹² You are the one who will profit if you have wisdom, and if you reject it you are the one who will suffer.

¹³ Stupidity is like a loud, ignorant, shameless woman.ᵍ ¹⁴ She sits at the door of her house, or on a seat in the highest part of town, ¹⁵ and calls out to people passing by, who are minding their own business: ¹⁶ "Come in, ignorant people!" She says to the foolish man, ¹⁷ "Stolen water is sweeter. Stolen bread tastes better." ¹⁸ Her victims do not know that the people who go there die, that those who have already entered are now deep in the land of the dead.ʰ

Solomon's Proverbs

10 A wise son makes his father proud of him; a foolish one brings his mother grief.

² What you get by dishonesty will do you no good, but honesty can save your life.

³ The Lord will not let a good man go hungry, but he will keep a wicked man from getting what he wants.

⁴ Being lazy will make you poor, but hard work will make you rich.

⁵ A sensible man gathers the crops when they are ready; it is a disgrace to sleep through the time of harvest.

ᵍ Hebrew unclear.   ʰ LAND OF THE DEAD: See 2.18.

⁶ A good man will receive blessings. A wicked man's words hide a violent nature.

⁷ A good man will be remembered as a blessing, but wicked men will soon be forgotten.

⁸ Sensible people follow good advice. People who talk foolishly will come to ruin.

⁹ An honest man is safe and secure, but dishonest men will be caught.

¹⁰ A man who holds back the truth causes trouble, but one who openly criticizes works for peace.'

¹¹ A good man's words are a fountain of life, but a wicked man's words hide a violent nature.

¹² Hate stirs up trouble, but love ignores all offenses.

¹³ Intelligent people talk sense, but stupid people need to be punished.

¹⁴ Wise men get all the knowledge they can. When a fool speaks, trouble is not far off.

¹⁵ Wealth protects the rich man; poverty destroys the poor.

¹⁶ A good man's reward is life, but sin leads only to more sin.

¹⁷ A man who listens when he is corrected will live, but a man who will not admit that he is wrong is in danger.

¹⁸ A man who tells lies is a man who hates. Anyone who spreads gossip is a fool.

¹⁹ The more you talk, the more likely you are to sin. If you are wise, you will keep quiet.

²⁰ A good man's words are like pure silver; a wicked man's ideas are worthless.

²¹ A good man's words will benefit many people, but you can kill yourself with stupidity.

²² The Lord's blessing makes a man wealthy. Hard work can make him no richer.

²³ A man is a fool to enjoy doing wrong. An intelligent man takes pleasure in wisdom.

²⁴ A righteous man gets what he wants, but a wicked man will get what he fears most.

²⁵ Storms come and the wicked are blown away, but honest men are always safe.

' *One ancient translation* but one . . . peace; *Hebrew repeats v. 8b.*

Anyone who spreads gossip is a fool

²⁶ Never get a lazy man to do something for you; he will be as irritating as vinegar on your teeth or smoke in your eyes.

²⁷ Fear the Lord and you will live longer. Wicked men die before their time.

²⁸ The hopes of good men lead to joy, but wicked people can look forward to nothing.

²⁹ The Lord protects innocent people, but destroys those who do wrong.

³⁰ Righteous people will always have security, but the wicked will not survive in the land.

³¹ Righteous men speak wisdom, but the tongue that speaks evil will be stopped.

³² Righteous men know the kind thing to say, but the wicked are always saying things that hurt.

11 The Lord hates people who use dishonest scales. He is happy with honest weights.

² Proud men will soon be disgraced. It is wiser to be modest.

³ Good men are guided by honesty. Those who can't be trusted are destroyed by their own dishonesty.

⁴ Riches will do you no good on the day you face death, but honesty can save your life.

⁵ Honesty makes a good man's life easier, but a wicked man will cause his own downfall.

⁶ Righteousness rescues the honest man, but a man who can't be trusted is trapped by his own greed.

⁷ When a wicked man dies, his hope dies with him. Confidence placed in riches comes to nothing.

⁸ The righteous man is protected from trouble; it comes to the wicked instead.

⁹ People are ruined by the talk of godless men, but saved by the wisdom of the righteous.

¹⁰ A city is happy when honest people have good fortune, and there are joyful shouts when wicked men die.

¹¹ Cities are made great by the presence of righteous men, but destroyed by the words of wicked men.

¹² It is foolish to speak scornfully to others. A smart man will keep quiet.

¹³ No one who gossips can be trusted with a secret, but you can put confidence in a trustworthy man.

¹⁴ A nation will fall if it has no guidance. Many advisers mean security.

¹⁵ Promise to pay a stranger's debt and you will regret it. You are better off if you don't get involved.

¹⁶ A gracious lady is respected, but a woman without virtue is a disgrace.

A lazy man will never have money,ʲ but an aggressive man will get rich.

¹⁷ You do yourself a favor when you are kind. If you are cruel, you only hurt yourself.

¹⁸ Wicked men do not really gain anything, but if you do what is right, you are certain to be rewarded.

¹⁹ A man who is determined to do right will live, but anyone who insists on doing wrong will die.

²⁰ The Lord hates evil-minded people, but is pleased with those who do right.

²¹ You can be sure that evil men will be punished, but righteous men will escape.

²² Beauty in a woman without good judgment is like a gold ring in a pig's snout.

²³ What good men want always results in good; when wicked men get what they want everyone is angry.

²⁴ Some people use their money freely, and still grow richer. Others are cautious, and yet grow poorer.

²⁵ Be generous and you will be prosperous. Help others and they will help you.

²⁶ People curse a man who hoards grain, waiting for a higher price, but they praise the one who puts it up for sale.

²⁷ If your goals are good, you will be respected, but if you are looking for trouble, that is what you will get.

²⁸ Those who depend on their wealth will fall like the leaves of autumn, but the righteous will prosper like the leaves of summer.

²⁹ The man who brings trouble on his family will have nothing at the end. Foolish men will always be servants to the wise.

³⁰ Righteousnessᵏ gives life, but violenceˡ takes it away.

³¹ A good man is rewarded here on earth; surely then wicked men and sinners will be punished.

ʲ *One ancient translation* but a woman . . . money; *Hebrew omits.*
ᵏ *One ancient translation* Righteousness; *Hebrew* A righteous man.
ˡ violence; *Hebrew* a wise man.

12 A man who loves knowledge wants to be told when he is wrong. It is stupid to hate being corrected.

2 The Lord is pleased with good men, but condemns those who plan evil.

3 Wickedness does not give security, but righteous men stand firm.

4 A good wife is her husband's pride and joy. But if she brings shame on him, she is like a cancer in his bones.

5 Honest men will treat you fairly; the wicked only want to deceive you.

6 The words of wicked men are murderous, but the words of the righteous rescue those who are threatened.

7 Wicked men meet their downfall and leave no descendants, but the families of righteous men live on.

8 If you are intelligent, you will be praised; if you are stupid, people will look down on you.

9 It is better to be an ordinary man working for a living, than to play the part of a great man but go hungry.

10 A good man takes care of his animals, but wicked men are cruel to theirs.

11 A hard-working farmer has plenty to eat, but it is stupid to waste time on useless projects.

12 All that wicked men want is to find evil things to do, but righteous men stand firm.^m

13 A wicked man is trapped by his own words, but an honest man gets himself out of trouble.

14 A man's reward depends on what he says and what he does; he will get what he deserves.

15 A stupid man thinks he is always right. Wise men listen to advice.

16 When a fool is annoyed, he quickly lets it be known. A smart man will ignore an insult.

17 When you tell the truth, justice is done, but lies lead to injustice.

18 Thoughtless words can wound as deeply as any sword, but the words of a wise man can heal.

19 A lie has a short life, but truth lives on forever.

20 Those who plan evil are in for a rude surprise, but those who work for good will find happiness.

21 Nothing bad happens to the righteous man, but wicked men get nothing but trouble.

m *Verse 12 in Hebrew is unclear.*

22 The Lord hates liars, but is pleased with those who keep their word.

23 A smart man will keep quiet about what he knows, but stupid people advertise their ignorance.

24 Hard work gives a man power; being lazy will make him a slave.

25 Worry can rob a man of happiness, but kind words will cheer him up.

26 A righteous man always examines his conduct,[n] but wicked men get lost along the way.

27 A lazy man will never get what he is after, but a hard-working man will get a fortune.[o]

28 Righteousness is the road to life; foolishness is the road to death.[p]

13 A wise son pays attention when his father corrects him, but an arrogant person never admits he is wrong.

2 Good men will be rewarded for what they say, but deceitful men are hungry for violence.

3 Be careful what you say, and protect your life. A careless talker destroys himself.

4 No matter how much a lazy man may want something, he will never get it. A hard worker will get everything he wants.

5 Honest people hate lies, but an evil man's words are shameful and disgraceful.

6 Righteousness protects the innocent. Wickedness is the downfall of sinners.

7 Some people pretend to be rich, but have nothing. Others pretend to be poor, but own a fortune.

8 A rich man has to use his money to save his life, but no one threatens a poor man.

9 The righteous are like a light shining brightly; the wicked are like a lamp flickering out.

10 Arrogance causes nothing but trouble. It is wiser to ask for advice.

11 The more easily you get your wealth, the sooner you will lose it. The harder it is to earn, the more you will have.

12 When hope is crushed, the heart is crushed, but a wish come true fills you with hope.

n examines his conduct; *Hebrew* spies out his neighbor.
o *Verse 27 in Hebrew is unclear.*   p *Verse 28 in Hebrew is unclear.*

¹³ Refuse good advice and you are asking for trouble; follow it, and you are safe.

¹⁴ The teachings of wise men are a fountain of life, they will help you escape when your life is in danger.

¹⁵ Intelligence wins respect, but men who can't be trusted are on the road to ruin.[q]

¹⁶ A sensible man always thinks before he acts, but a stupid man advertises his ignorance.

¹⁷ Unreliable messengers cause trouble, but those who can be trusted make peace.

¹⁸ A man who will not learn will be poor and disgraced. One who listens to correction is respected.

¹⁹ How good it is to get what you want!

Stupid people refuse to turn away from evil.

²⁰ Learn from wise men and you will become wise. Make friends with stupid people and you will be ruined.

²¹ Trouble follows sinners everywhere, but righteous men will be rewarded with good things.

²² A good man will have wealth to leave to his grandchildren, but the wealth of sinners will go to righteous men.

²³ Unused fields could yield plenty of food for the poor, but unjust men keep them from being farmed.[r]

²⁴ If you don't punish your son, you don't love him. If you do love him, you will correct him.

²⁵ Righteous men have enough to eat, but wicked men are always hungry.

14 Homes are made by the wisdom of women, but are destroyed by foolishness.

² Be honest, and you show that you fear the Lord; be dishonest, and you show that you do not.

³ A fool's pride makes him talk too much; a wise man's words protect him.

⁴ Without any animals to pull the plow you may grow a little grain, but with them you can grow much more.

⁵ A reliable witness always tells the truth, but an unreliable one tells nothing but lies.

⁶ A conceited man can never become wise, but an intelligent man learns easily.

⁷ Stay away from foolish people; they have nothing to teach you.

---

q road to ruin; *Hebrew* permanent road.
r *Verse 23 in Hebrew is unclear.*

⁸ Why is a clever man wise? Because he knows what to do. Why is a stupid man foolish? Because he only thinks he knows.

⁹ Foolish people don't care if they sin, but good people want to be forgiven.*

¹⁰ Your joy is your own; your bitterness is your own. No one can share them with you.

¹¹ A good man's house will still be standing after an evil man's house has been destroyed.

¹² What you think is the right road may lead to death.

¹³ A man's laughter may hide his sadness. When happiness is gone, sorrow is always there.

¹⁴ A bad man will get what he deserves. A good man will be rewarded for his deeds.ᵗ

¹⁵ A fool will believe anything; a smart man watches his step.

¹⁶ A sensible man is careful to stay out of trouble, but a stupid man is careless and acts too quickly.

¹⁷ A man with a hot temper does foolish things; a wiser man remains calm.ᵘ

¹⁸ Ignorant people get what their foolishness deserves, but the clever are rewarded with knowledge.

¹⁹ Evil men will have to bow down to the righteous, and humbly beg their favor.

²⁰ No one likes a poor man, but the rich have many friends.

²¹ If you want to be happy, be kind to the poor; it is a sin to despise anyone.

²² You will earn the trust and respect of others if you work for good; if you work for evil, you make a fatal mistake.

²³ Work, and you will earn a living; sit around talking, and you will be poor.

²⁴ Wise men are rewarded with wealth, but a fool is known byᵛ his foolishness.

²⁵ A witness saves lives when he tells the truth; when he tells lies he betrays people.

²⁶ True religion gives confidence and security to a man and his family.

ˢ *Verse 9 in Hebrew is unclear.*
ᵗ for his deeds; *Hebrew from upon him.*
ᵘ *One ancient translation remains calm; Hebrew is hated.*
ᵛ is known by; *Hebrew unclear.*

²⁷ Do you want to avoid death? True religion is a fountain of life.

²⁸ A king's greatness depends on how many people he rules; without them he is nothing.

²⁹ A man who stays calm is wise, but a man with a hot temper only shows how stupid he is.

³⁰ Peace of mind makes the body healthy, but jealousy is like a cancer.

³¹ Oppress a poor man, and you insult the God who made him; but kindness shown to the poor is an act of worship.

³² A wicked man's evil deeds bring about his own downfall, but a good man is protected by his integrity.^w

³³ Wisdom is in every thought of an intelligent man; fools know nothing about wisdom.

³⁴ Righteousness makes a nation great; sin is a disgrace to any nation.

³⁵ Kings are pleased with competent officials, but they punish those who fail them.

15 A gentle answer quiets anger, but a harsh one stirs it up.

² When a wise man speaks, he makes knowledge attractive, but stupid men spout nonsense.

³ The Lord sees what happens everywhere; he is watching us, whether we do good or evil.

⁴ Kind words bring life, but cruel words crush a man's spirit.

⁵ It is foolish to ignore what your father taught you; it is wise to accept his correction.

⁶ Righteous men keep their wealth, but wicked men lose theirs when hard times come.

⁷ Knowledge is spread by wise men, not by fools.

⁸ The Lord is pleased when good men pray, but hates the sacrifices that wicked men bring him.

⁹ The Lord hates the ways of evil men, but loves a man who does what is right.

¹⁰ If you do what is wrong, you will be severely punished; you will die if you do not let yourself be corrected.

^w *Some ancient translations* integrity; *Hebrew* death.

¹¹ Not even the world of the dead* can keep the Lord from knowing what is there; how then can a man hide his thoughts from God?

¹² A conceited man does not like to be corrected; he never asks wise men for advice.

¹³ When a man is happy he smiles, but when he is sad he looks depressed.

¹⁴ An intelligent man wants to learn, but stupid people are satisfied with ignorance.

¹⁵ The life of a poor man is a constant struggle, but happy people always enjoy life.

¹⁶ Better to be poor and fear the Lord, than to be rich and in trouble.

¹⁷ Better to eat vegetables with people you love, than to eat the finest meat where there is hate.

¹⁸ Hot tempers cause arguments, but patience brings peace.

¹⁹ If you are lazy you will meet difficulty everywhere, but if you are honest you will have no trouble.

²⁰ A wise son makes his father happy. Only a fool despises his mother.

²¹ Stupid people are happy with their foolishness, but a wise man will do what is right.

²² Get all the advice you can and you will succeed; without it you will fail.

²³ What a joy it is to find just the right word for the right occasion!

²⁴ A wise man walks up the road to life, not down the road to death.

²⁵ The Lord will destroy the homes of arrogant men, but he will protect a widow's property.

²⁶ The Lord hates the thoughts of evil men, but he is pleased with friendly words.

²⁷ Try to make profit dishonestly, and you get your family in trouble. Don't take bribes, and you will live longer.

²⁸ Good men think before they answer. Evil men have a quick reply, but it causes trouble.

²⁹ When good men pray the Lord listens, but he ignores evil men.

³⁰ Smiling faces make you happy, and good news makes you feel better.

*WORLD OF THE DEAD: See 2.18.

³¹ If you pay attention when you are corrected, you are a wise man.

³² If you refuse to learn you are hurting yourself. If you accept correction you will become wiser.

³³ True religion is an education in itself. You must be humble before you can ever receive honors.

16 Men may make their plans, but God has the last word.

² You may think everything you do is right, but the Lord judges your motives.

³ Ask the Lord to bless your plans, and you will be successful in carrying them out.

⁴ Everything the Lord has made has its destiny; and the destiny of the wicked man is destruction.

⁵ The Lord hates everyone who is arrogant; he will never let them escape punishment.

⁶ Be loyal and faithful and God will forgive your sin. Fear the Lord and nothing evil will happen to you.

⁷ When you please the Lord, you can make your enemies into friends.

⁸ It is better to have a little, honestly earned, than to have a large income, gained dishonestly.

⁹ You may make your plans, but God directs your actions.

¹⁰ The king speaks with divine authority; his decisions are always right.

¹¹ The Lord wants weights and measures to be honest, and every sale to be fair.

¹² Kings cannot tolerate evil, because justice is what makes a government strong.

¹³ A king wants to hear the truth, and will favor men who speak it.

¹⁴ A wise man will try to keep the king happy; if the king becomes angry, someone may die.

¹⁵ The king's favor is like the clouds that bring rain in the springtime—life is there.

¹⁶ It is better—much better—to have wisdom and knowledge than gold and silver.

¹⁷ Good men travel a road that avoids evil; so watch where you are going—it may save your life.

¹⁸ Pride leads to destruction, and arrogance to downfall.

Every sale to be fair

[19] It is better to be one of the poor and humble, than one of the arrogant and get a share of their loot.

[20] Pay attention to what you are taught, and you will be successful; trust in the Lord, and you will be happy.

[21] A wise, mature man is known for his understanding. The more pleasant his words, the more persuasive he is.

[22] Wisdom is a fountain of life to the wise, but it is a waste of time to try to educate stupid people.

[23] A wise man thinks before he speaks; what he says is then more persuasive.

[24] Kind words are like honey—sweet to the taste and good for your health.

[25] What you think is the right road may lead to death.

[26] A laborer's appetite makes him work harder, because he wants to satisfy his hunger.

[27] An evil man looks for ways to harm others; even his words burn with evil.

[28] Wicked men spread gossip; they stir up trouble and break up friendships.

[29] A man of violence deceives his friends and leads them to disaster.

[30] Watch out for people who grin and wink at you; they have thought of something evil.

[31] Long life is a righteous man's reward; his gray hair is a glorious crown.

[32] It is better to be patient than powerful. It is better to win control over yourself than over whole cities.

[33] Men roll the sacred dice[y] to learn God's will, but God himself determines the answer.

17 Better to eat a dry crust of bread with peace of mind than have a banquet in a house full of trouble.

[2] A shrewd servant will gain authority over his master's worthless son, and receive a part of the inheritance.

[3] Gold and silver are tested by fire, and a person's heart is tested by the Lord.

[4] Evil men listen to evil ideas and liars listen to lies.

[5] Make fun of a poor man and you insult the God who made him. You will be punished if you take pleasure in someone's misfortune.

[6] Old men are proud of their grandchildren, just as boys are proud of their fathers.

[y] SACRED DICE: Specially marked stones were used to determine God's will.

⁷ A respected man does not tell a lie, any more than a fool says something worthwhile.

⁸ Some people think a bribe works like magic; they believe it can do anything.

⁹ If you want people to like you, forgive them when they wrong you. Remembering wrongs can break up a friendship.

¹⁰ An intelligent man learns more from one rebuke than a fool learns from being beaten a hundred times.

¹¹ Death will come like a cruel messenger to evil men who are always stirring up trouble.

¹² It is better to meet a mother bear robbed of her cubs than to meet some fool busy with a stupid project.

¹³ If you repay good with evil, you will never get evil out of your house.

¹⁴ The start of an argument is like the first break in a dam; stop it before it goes any further.

¹⁵ Condemning the innocent or letting the wicked go—both are hateful to the Lord.

¹⁶ It does a fool no good to spend money on an education, because he has no common sense.

¹⁷ Friends always show their love. What are brothers for if not to share trouble?

¹⁸ Only a man with no sense would promise to be responsible for his neighbor's debts.

¹⁹ To like sin is to like making trouble. A man who brags all the time is asking for trouble.

²⁰ A man who thinks and speaks evil can expect to find nothing good—only disaster.

²¹ There is nothing but sadness and sorrow for a father whose son does foolish things.

²² Being cheerful keeps you healthy. It is slow death to be gloomy all the time.

²³ Corrupt judges accept secret bribes, and then justice is not done.

²⁴ A mature man knows the wise thing to do, but an immature person can never decide.

²⁵ A foolish son brings grief to his father, and bitter regrets to his mother.

²⁶ It is not right to make an innocent man pay a fine; justice is perverted when good men are beaten.

²⁷ A man who is sure of himself does not talk all the time. A man who stays calm has real insight. ²⁸ After all, even a fool may be thought wise and intelligent if he stays quiet and keeps his mouth shut.

18 A man who does not get along with other people is interested only in himself; he will disagree with what everyone else knows is right.

² A fool does not care whether he understands a thing or not; all he wants to do is show how smart he is.

³ Sin and shame go together. Lose your honor and you will get scorn in its place.

⁴ Human language can be a source of wisdom, deep as the ocean, fresh as a flowing stream.

⁵ It is not right to favor the guilty and keep the innocent from receiving justice.

⁶ When some fool starts an argument, he is asking for a beating.

⁷ When a fool speaks, he is ruining himself; he gets caught in the trap of his own words.

⁸ Gossip is so tasty—how we love to swallow it!

⁹ A lazy man is as bad as someone who tears things down.

¹⁰ The name of the Lord is like a strong tower, where a righteous man can go and be safe.

¹¹ Rich people imagine that their wealth protects them like high, strong walls around a city.

¹² No one is respected unless he is humble; an arrogant man is on the way to ruin.

¹³ Listen before you answer. If you don't, you are being stupid and insulting.

¹⁴ A man's will to live can sustain him when he is sick, but if he loses it, his last hope is gone.

¹⁵ Intelligent people are always eager and ready to learn.

¹⁶ Do you want to meet an important person? Take him a gift and it will be easy.

¹⁷ The first man to speak in court always seems right until his opponent begins to question him.

¹⁸ If two powerful men are opposing each other in court, the sacred dice*ᶻ* can settle the issue.

ᶻ SACRED DICE: See 16.33.

¹⁹ Help your brother and he will protect you like a strong city wall,ᵃ but if you quarrel with him he will close his doors to you.

²⁰ You will have to live with the consequences of everything you say. ²¹ What you say can preserve life or destroy it; so you must accept the consequences of your words.

²² Find a wife and you find a good thing; it shows that the Lord is good to you.

²³ When the poor man speaks, he begs, but when the rich man answers, he is rude.

²⁴ Some friendships doᵇ not last; but some friends are more loyal than brothers.

19   It is better to be poor but honest than to be a lying fool.

² Enthusiasm without knowledge is not good; impatience will get you into trouble.

³ Some people ruin themselves by their own stupid actions, and then blame the Lord.

⁴ Rich people are always finding new friends, but the poor cannot keep the few they have.

⁵ Tell lies in court and you will be punished—there will be no escape.

⁶ Everyone tries to gain the favor of important people; everyone claims the friendship of a man who gives out favors.

⁷ The brothers of a poor man have no use for him; no wonder he has no friends. No matter how hard he tries, he cannot win any.ᶜ

⁸ Do yourself a favor and learn all you can; then remember what you learn and you will prosper.

⁹ No one who tells lies in court can escape punishment; he is doomed.

¹⁰ Fools should not live in luxury, and slaves should not rule over noblemen.

¹¹ A sensible man keeps his temper. When someone wrongs you, it is a great virtue to ignore it.

¹² The king's anger is like the roar of a lion, but his favor is like welcome rain.

¹³ A stupid son can bring his father to ruin. A nagging wife is like water going drip-drip-drip.

ᵃ *Some ancient translations* Help . . . wall; *Hebrew unclear.*
ᵇ *Some ancient translations* Some friendships do; *Hebrew* A man of friends does.
ᶜ No matter . . . any; *Hebrew unclear.*

¹⁴ A man can inherit a home and money from his parents, but only the Lord can give him a sensible wife.

¹⁵ Go ahead and be lazy; sleep on, but you will go hungry.

¹⁶ Keep God's laws and you will live longer; ignore them and you will die.

¹⁷ When you give to the poor it is like lending to the Lord, because the Lord will pay you back.

¹⁸ Discipline your children while they are young enough to learn. If you don't, you are helping them destroy themselves.

¹⁹ If a man has a hot temper, let him take the consequences. If you get him out of trouble once, you will have to do it again.

²⁰ Listen to advice and be willing to learn, and one day you will be wise.

²¹ A man may plan all kinds of things, but the Lord's will is going to be done.

²² It is a disgrace to be greedy; a poor man is better off than a liar.

²³ Fear the Lord, and you will live a long life, content and safe from harm.

²⁴ Some people are too lazy to put food in their own mouths.

²⁵ Arrogance should be punished, so that people who don't know any better can learn a lesson. A wise man will learn when he is corrected.

²⁶ Only a shameful, disgraceful person would mistreat his father, or turn his mother away from his home.

²⁷ Son, when you stop learning, you will soon neglect what you already know.

²⁸ There is no justice where a witness is determined to hurt someone. Wicked men love the taste of evil.

²⁹ A conceited fool is sure to get a beating.

20 Drinking too much makes you loud and foolish. It's stupid to get drunk.

² Fear an angry king as you would a growling lion; making him angry is suicide.

³ Any fool can start arguments; the honorable thing is to stay out of them.

⁴ A farmer too lazy to plow his fields at the right time will have nothing to harvest.

⁵ A man's thoughts are like water in a deep well, but someone with insight can draw them out.

⁶ Everyone talks about how loyal and faithful he is, but just try to find someone who really is!

⁷ Children are fortunate if they have a father who is honest and does what is right.

⁸ The king sits in judgment, and knows evil when he sees it.

⁹ Can anyone really say that his conscience is clear, that he has gotten rid of his sin?

¹⁰ The Lord hates those who use dishonest weights and measures.

¹¹ A child shows what he is by what he does; you can tell if he is honest and good.

¹² The Lord has given us eyes to see with, and ears to listen with.

¹³ Spend your time sleeping, and you will be poor. Keep busy, and you will have plenty to eat.

¹⁴ The customer always complains that the price is too high, but then he goes off and brags about the bargain he got.

¹⁵ If you know what you are talking about, you have something more valuable than gold or jewels.

¹⁶ Anyone stupid enough to promise to be responsible for a stranger's debts ought to have his own property held to guarantee payment.

¹⁷ What you get by dishonesty you may enjoy like the finest food, but sooner or later it will be like a mouthful of sand.

¹⁸ Get good advice and you will succeed; don't go charging into battle without a plan.

¹⁹ A gossip can never keep a secret. Stay away from someone who talks too much.

²⁰ If you curse your parents, your life will end like a lamp that goes out in the dark.

²¹ The more easily you get your wealth, the less good it will do you.

²² Don't take it on yourself to repay a wrong. Trust the Lord and he will make it right.

²³ The Lord hates people who use dishonest scales and weights.

²⁴ The Lord has determined our path; how then can anyone understand his own life?

²⁵ Think carefully before you promise an offering to God. You might regret it later.

²⁶ A wise king will find out who is doing wrong, and punish him without pity.

²⁷ The Lord gave us mind and conscience; we cannot hide from ourselves.

²⁸ A king will remain in power as long as his rule is honest, just, and fair.

²⁹ We admire the strength of youth, and respect the gray hair of age.

³⁰ Sometimes it takes a painful experience to make us change our ways.

21 The Lord controls the mind of a king as easily as he directs the course of a stream.

² Even though you think everything you do is right, remember that the Lord judges your motives.

³ Do what is right and fair; that pleases the Lord more than bringing him sacrifices.

⁴ Wicked people are controlled by their conceit and arrogance, and this is sinful.

⁵ Plan carefully and you will have plenty; act too quickly and you will never have enough.

⁶ The riches you get by dishonesty soon disappear, but not before they lead you into the jaws of death.

⁷ The wicked are doomed by their own violence; they refuse to do what is right.

⁸ Guilty men walk a crooked path; innocent men do what is right.

⁹ Better to live in the attic than share the house with a nagging wife.

¹⁰ Wicked people are always hungry for evil; they have no mercy on anyone.

¹¹ When a conceited man gets his punishment, even an unthinking person learns a lesson. A wise man will learn from what he is taught.

¹² A righteous man knows what evil men are thinking,ᵈ and so can cause their ruin.

ᵈ *One ancient translation* what evil men are thinking; *Hebrew* the house of evil men.

[13] Refuse to listen to the cry of the poor, and your own cry for help will not be heard.

[14] If someone is angry with you, a gift given secretly will calm him down.

[15] When justice is done, good men are happy and evil men are brought to despair.

[16] Death waits for the man who wanders away from good sense.

[17] Indulging in luxuries, wine, and rich food will never make you wealthy.

[18] Wicked men bring on themselves the suffering they try to cause good men.

[19] Better to live out in the desert than with a nagging, complaining wife.

[20] Wise men live in wealth and luxury, but stupid men spend their money as fast as they get it.

[21] Be kind and honest, and you will live a long life; others will respect you and treat you fairly.

[22] A shrewd general can take a city defended by strong men, and destroy the walls they relied on.

[23] If you want to stay out of trouble, be careful what you say.

[24] Show me a conceited person and I will show you someone who is arrogant, proud, and inconsiderate.

[25] A lazy man who refuses to work is only killing himself; [26] all he does is think about what he would like to have. A righteous man, however, can give, and give generously.

[27] The Lord hates it when wicked men offer him sacrifices, especially if they do it from evil motives.

[28] The testimony of a liar is not believed, but the word of a man who thinks things through is accepted.

[29] A righteous man is sure of himself; a wicked man has to pretend as best he can.

[30] Wisdom, brilliance, insight—they are nothing in the Lord's sight.

[31] You can get horses ready for battle, but it is the Lord who gives victory.

22 If you have to choose between a good reputation and great wealth, choose a good reputation.

[2] There is no difference between the rich and the poor, because the Lord made them both.

Your own cry for help will not be heard

³ A sensible man will see trouble coming and avoid it, but an unthinking person will go right on and regret it later.

⁴ Fear the Lord, be humble, and you will get riches, honor, and a long life.

⁵ If you love your life, stay away from the traps that catch the wicked along the way.

⁶ Teach a child how he should live, and he will remember it all his life.

⁷ Poor people are the rich man's slaves. Borrow money and you are the lender's slave.

⁸ Plant the seeds of injustice, and disaster will spring up, a furious punishment that will destroy you.ᵉ

⁹ Be generous, and share your food with the poor. You will be blessed for it.

¹⁰ Get rid of a conceited person, and then argument, quarreling, and name-calling will stop.

¹¹ You can win the friendship of kings with flattery, but the Lordᶠ loves a person who is sincere.

¹² The Lord sees to it that truth is kept safe by disproving the words of liars.

¹³ The lazy man stays at home; he says a lion might get him if he goes outside.

¹⁴ Adultery is a trap—it catches those with whom the Lord is angry.

¹⁵ Children just naturally do silly, careless things, but a good spanking will teach them how to behave.

¹⁶ If you make gifts to rich people, or oppress the poor to get rich, you will become poor yourself.

The Thirty Wise Sayings

¹⁷ Listen, and I will teach you what wise men have said. Study their teachings, ¹⁸ and you will be glad if you remember them and can quote them. ¹⁹ I want you to put your trust in the Lord; that is why I am going to tell them to you now. ²⁰ I have written down thirty sayings for you. They contain knowledge and good advice, ²¹ and will teach you what the truth really is. Then when you are sent to find it out, you will bring back the right answer.ᵍ

ᵉ destroy you; *Hebrew* come to an end.
ᶠ *One ancient translation* the Lord; *Hebrew omits.*
ᵍ *Verse 21 in Hebrew is unclear.*

-1-

²² Don't take advantage of poor men just because you can; don't take advantage of men who stand helpless in court. ²³ The Lord will argue their case for them, and threaten the life of anyone who threatens theirs.

-2-

²⁴ Don't make friends with people who have hot, violent tempers. ²⁵ You might learn their habits, and not be able to change.

-3-

²⁶ Don't promise to be responsible for someone else's debts. ²⁷ If you should be unable to pay, they will take away even your bed.

-4-

²⁸ Never move an old property line that your ancestors established.

-5-

²⁹ Show me a man who does a good job, and I will show you a man who is better than most, and worthy of the company of kings.

-6-

23 When you sit down to eat with an important man, keep in mind who he is. ² If you have a big appetite, restrain yourself. ³ Don't be greedy for the fine food he serves; he may be trying to trick you.

-7-

⁴ Be wise enough not to wear yourself out trying to get rich. ⁵ Your money can be gone in a flash, as if it had grown wings and flown away like an eagle.

-8-

⁶ Don't eat at the table of a stingy man, or be greedy for the fine food he serves. ⁷ "Come on and have some more," he says, but he doesn't mean it. His attitude will make you[h] sick; ⁸ you will vomit up what you have eaten, and all your flattery will be wasted.

-9-

⁹ Don't try to talk sense to a fool; he can't appreciate it.

[h] you; *Hebrew* him.

–10–

¹⁰ Never move an old property line, or take over land owned by orphans. ¹¹ The Lord is their powerful defender, and he will argue their case against you.

–11–

¹² Pay attention to your teacher and learn all you can.

–12–

¹³ Don't hesitate to discipline a child. A good beating won't kill him. ¹⁴ As a matter of fact, it may save his life.

–13–

¹⁵ Son, if you become wise, I will be very happy. ¹⁶ I will be proud when I hear you speaking words of wisdom.

–14–

¹⁷ Don't be envious of sinful men; let your religion be the concern of your life. ¹⁸ If it is, you have a bright future.

–15–

¹⁹ Listen, my son, be wise, and give serious thought to the way you live. ²⁰ Don't associate with people who drink too much wine, or stuff themselves with food. ²¹ Drunkards and gluttons will be reduced to poverty. If all you do is eat and sleep, you will soon be wearing rags.

–16–

²² Listen to your father; without him you would not exist. When your mother is old, show her your appreciation. ²³ Truth, wisdom, learning, and good sense—these are worth paying for, but too valuable for you to sell. ²⁴ A righteous man's father has good reason to be happy. You can take pride in a wise son. ²⁵ Let your father and mother be proud of you; give your mother that happiness.

–17–

²⁶ Pay close attention, son, and let my life be your example. ²⁷ Prostitutes and immoral women are a deadly trap. ²⁸ They wait for you like robbers, and cause many men to be unfaithful.

–18–

²⁹⁻³⁰ Show me someone who drinks too much, who has to try out fancy drinks, and I will show you someone miser-

able and sorry for himself, always causing trouble and always complaining. His eyes are bloodshot and he has bruises that could have been avoided. 31 Don't let wine tempt you, even though it is rich red, and you can see yourself in the cup, and it looks so good as you swish it around. 32 The next morning you will feel as if you have been bitten by a poisonous snake. 33 Weird sights will appear before your eyes, and you will not be able to think or speak clearly. 34 You will feel as if you were out on the ocean, seasick, swinging high up in the rigging of a tossing ship. 35 "I must have been hit," you will say; "I must have been beaten up, but I don't remember it. Why can't I wake up? I need another drink."

–19–

24 Don't be envious of evil men, and don't try to make friends with them. 2 All they think about is causing trouble; every time they open their mouths someone is going to be hurt.

–20–

3 Homes are built on the foundation of wisdom and understanding. 4 Where there is knowledge, the rooms are furnished with valuable, beautiful things.

–21–

5 Being wise is better than being strong;' yes, knowledge is more important than strength. 6 After all, you must make careful plans before you fight a battle, and the more good advice you get, the more likely you are to win.

–22–

7 Wise sayings are too deep for a stupid person to understand. He has nothing to say when important matters are being discussed.

–23–

8 If you are always planning evil, you will earn a reputation as a troublemaker. 9 Any scheme a fool thinks up is sinful. People hate a man who has nothing but scorn for others.

–24–

10 If you are weak in a crisis, you are weak indeed.

' *Some ancient translations* Being wise is better than being strong; *Hebrew* A man is wise in strength.

–25–

¹¹ Don't hesitate to rescue a man being dragged away to his execution. ¹² You may say that it is none of your business, but God knows and judges your motives. He keeps watch on you; he knows. And he pays men back for what they do.

–26–

¹³ Son, eat honey; it is good. And just as honey from the comb is sweet on your tongue, ¹⁴ knowledge and wisdom are good for the soul. Get them, and you have a bright future.

–27–

¹⁵ Don't make schemes to rob an honest man or to take away his home; it is evil. ¹⁶ No matter how often an honest man falls, he always gets up again. But disaster destroys the wicked.

–28–

¹⁷ Don't be glad when your enemy meets disaster. ¹⁸ The Lord will know if you are, and will not like it. Then he may not punish him.

–29–

¹⁹ Don't let evil men worry you; don't be envious of them. ²⁰ A wicked man has no future—nothing to look forward to.

–30–

²¹ Fear the Lord, my son, and fear the king. Have nothing to do with people who rebel against them; ²² such men could be ruined in a moment. Do you realize the disaster that God, or the king, can cause?

More Wise Sayings

²³ Wise men have also said these things:

It is wrong for a judge to be prejudiced. ²⁴ If he pronounces a guilty man innocent, he will be cursed and hated by everyone in the world. ²⁵ Judges who punish the guilty, however, will be prosperous and enjoy a good reputation.

²⁶ An honest answer is a sign of true friendship.

²⁷ Don't build your house and establish a home until your fields are ready, and you are sure that you can earn a living.

²⁸ Don't give evidence against a neighbor without good reason, or say misleading things about him. ²⁹ Don't say, "I'll do to him just what he did to me! I'll get even with him!"

³⁰ I walked through the fields and vineyards of a lazy, stupid man. ³¹ They were full of thorn bushes, and overgrown with weeds. The stone wall around them had fallen down. ³² I looked at this, thought about it, and learned a lesson from it: ³³ Go ahead and take your nap; go ahead and sleep. Fold your hands and rest awhile, ³⁴ but while you are asleep, poverty will attack you like an armed robber.

More of Solomon's Proverbs

25 Here are more of Solomon's proverbs, copied by men at the court of King Hezekiah of Judah.

² We honor God for what he conceals; we honor kings for what they explain.

³ You never know what a king is thinking; his thoughts are beyond us, like the heights of the sky, or the depths of the ocean.

⁴ Take the impurities out of silver, and the artist can produce a thing of beauty. ⁵ Keep evil advisers away from the king, and his government will be known for its justice.

⁶ When you stand before the king, don't try to impress him and pretend to be important. ⁷ It is better to be asked to take a higher position than to be told to give your place to someone more important.

⁸ Don't be too quick to go to court about something you have seen. If another witness later proves you wrong, what will you do then?

⁹ If you and your neighbor have a difference of opinion, settle it between yourselves and do not reveal any secrets. ¹⁰ Otherwise everyone will learn that you can't keep a secret, and you will never live down the shame.

¹¹ An idea well-expressed is like a design of gold, set in silver.

¹² A warning given by an experienced man to someone willing to listen is more valuable than gold rings, or jewelry made of the finest gold.

¹³ A reliable messenger is refreshing to the one who sends him, like cold water in the heat of harvest time.

¹⁴ People who promise things that they never give are like clouds and wind that bring no rain.

¹⁵ Patient persuasion can break down the strongest resistance, and even convince rulers.

¹⁶ Never eat more honey than you need; too much may make you vomit. ¹⁷ Don't visit your neighbor too often; he may get tired of you, and come to hate you.

¹⁸ A man who tells lies about his neighbor is as deadly as a sword, a club, or a sharp arrow.

¹⁹ Relying on an undependable person in a crisis is like trying to chew with a loose tooth, or walk with a crippled foot. ²⁰ You might as well try to keep warm on a cold day by taking your clothes off.

Singing to a person who is depressed is like rubbing salt in a wound.

²¹ If your enemy is hungry, feed him; if he is thirsty, give him a drink. ²² You will make him burn with shame, and the Lord will reward you.

²³ Gossip brings anger, just as surely as the north wind brings rain.

²⁴ Better to live in the attic than share the house with a nagging wife.

²⁵ Hearing good news that you did not expect is like a drink of cold water when you are dry and thirsty.

²⁶ A good man who gives in to an evil man reminds you of a polluted spring, or a poisoned well.

²⁷ Too much honey is bad for you, and so is trying to win too much praise.ʲ

²⁸ If you cannot control your anger, you are as helpless as a city without walls, open to attack.

26 Praise for a fool is out of place, like snow in summer, or rain at harvest time.

² Curses cannot hurt you unless you deserve them. They are like birds that fly by and never light.

³ You have to whip a horse, you have to bridle a donkey, and you have to beat a fool.

⁴ If you answer a silly question, you are just as silly as the person who asked it.

⁵ Give a silly answer to a silly question, and the one who asked it will realize that he's not as smart as he thinks.

ʲ and so . . . praise; *Hebrew unclear.*

⁶ A man who lets a fool deliver a message might as well cut off his own feet; he is asking for trouble.

⁷ A fool can use a proverb as well as a crippled man can use his legs.

⁸ Praising a stupid man makes as much sense as tying a rock in a slingshot.

⁹ A fool quoting a wise saying reminds you of a drunk man trying to pick a thorn out of his hand.

¹⁰ An employer who hires any fool that comes along is only hurting everybody concerned.*

¹¹ A fool doing some stupid thing a second time is like a dog going back to its vomit.

¹² The most stupid fool is better off than someone who thinks he is wise when he is not.

¹³ Why doesn't the lazy man ever get out of the house? What is he afraid of? Lions?

¹⁴ The lazy man turns over in bed. He's like a door swinging on its hinges—really going places.

¹⁵ Some people are too lazy to put food in their own mouths.

¹⁶ A lazy man will think he is smarter than seven men who can give good reasons for their opinions.

¹⁷ Getting involved in an argument that is none of your business is like going down the street and grabbing a dog by the ears.

¹⁸⁻¹⁹ A man who tricks someone and then claims that he was only joking is like a crazy man playing with a deadly weapon.

²⁰ Without wood, a fire goes out; without gossip, an argument stops.

²¹ Charcoal keeps the embers glowing, wood keeps the fire burning, and troublemakers keep arguments alive.

²² Gossip is so tasty! How we love to swallow it!

²³ Insincere* talk that hides what you are really thinking is like a fine glaze* on a cheap clay pot.

²⁴ A hypocrite hides his hate behind flattering words. ²⁵ They may sound fine, but don't believe him, because his heart is filled to the brim with hate. ²⁶ He may disguise his hatred, but everyone will see the evil things he does.

k Verse 10 in Hebrew is unclear.
l One ancient translation Insincere; Hebrew Burning.
m fine glaze; Hebrew unrefined silver.

²⁷ People who set traps for others get caught themselves. People who start landslides get crushed.

²⁸ You have to hate someone to want to hurt him with lies. Insincere talk brings nothing but ruin.

27 Never boast about tomorrow. You don't know what will happen between now and then.

² Let other people praise you—even strangers; never do it yourself.

³ The weight of stone and sand is nothing compared to the trouble that stupidity can cause.

⁴ Anger is cruel and destructive, but it is nothing compared to jealousy.

⁵ Better to correct someone openly, than to let him think you don't care for him at all.

⁶ A friend means well, even when he hurts you. But when an enemy puts his arm around your shoulder—watch out!

⁷ When a man is full, he will refuse honey, but when he is hungry, even bitter food tastes sweet.

⁸ A man away from home is like a bird away from its nest.

⁹ Perfume and fragrant oils make you feel happier, and a close friendship makes you feel stronger.ⁿ

¹⁰ Do not forget your friends, or your father's friends. If you are in trouble, don't ask your brother for help; a nearby neighbor can help you more than a brother who is far away.

¹¹ Be wise, son, and I will be happy; I will have an answer for anyone who criticizes me.

¹² A sensible man will see trouble coming and avoid it, but the average person will go right on, and regret it later.

¹³ Anyone stupid enough to promise to be responsible for a stranger's debtsᵒ ought to have his own property held to guarantee payment.

¹⁴ You might as well curse your friend as wake him up early in the morning with a loud greeting.

¹⁵ A nagging wife is like a dreary day when the rain never stops. ¹⁶ How can you keep her quiet? Have you

ⁿ and a close . . . stronger; *Hebrew unclear.*
ᵒ *One ancient translation* stranger's debts; *Hebrew adds* or those of an immoral woman.

Take care of a fig tree

ever tried to stop the wind, or ever tried to hold a handful of oil?*

¹⁷ People learn from people, just as iron sharpens iron.

¹⁸ Take care of a fig tree and you will have figs to eat. A servant who takes care of his master will be honored.

¹⁹ It is your own face that you see reflected in the water, and it is your own self that you see in your heart.

²⁰ A man's desires are like the world of the dead*—there is always room for more.

²¹Fire tests gold and silver; a man's reputation can also be tested.

²² Even if you beat a fool half to death, he will still be as foolish as ever.

²³ Look after your sheep and cattle as carefully as you can, ²⁴ because wealth does not last forever. Not even nations do that. ²⁵ You cut the hay, and then cut the grass on the hillsides while the next crop of hay is growing. ²⁶ You can make clothes from the wool of your sheep, and buy land with the money you get from selling some of your goats. ²⁷ The rest of the goats will provide milk for you and your family, and for your servant girls as well.

28 Wicked men run when no one is chasing them, but an honest man is as brave as a lion.

² A nation will be strong and endure when it has intelligent, sensible leaders. But when a nation sins, it will have one ruler after another.

³ A man in authority who oppresses poor people is like a driving rain that destroys the crops.

⁴ If you have no regard for the law you are on the side of the wicked, but if you obey it you are against them.

⁵ Evil men do not know what justice is, but those who worship the Lord understand it well.

⁶ Better to be poor and honest than rich and dishonest.

⁷ A young man who obeys the law is intelligent. One who makes friends with good-for-nothings is a disgrace to his father.

⁸ If you get rich by charging interest and taking advantage of people, your wealth will go to someone who is kind to the poor.

⁹ If you do not obey the law, God will find your prayers too hateful to hear.

---

p or ever . . . oil; *Hebrew unclear.*   *q* WORLD OF THE DEAD: See 2.18.

¹⁰ Trick an honest man into doing evil and you will fall into your own trap.

The innocent will be rewarded well.

¹¹ Rich people always think they are wise, but a poor man with insight into character knows better.

¹² When good men come to power, everybody celebrates, but when bad men rule, people stay in hiding.

¹³ You will never succeed in life if you try to hide your sins. Confess them and repent; then God will show mercy to you.

¹⁴ Always fear the Lord and you will be happy. Be stubborn and you will be ruined.

¹⁵ Poor people are helpless against a wicked ruler; he is as dangerous as a growling lion, or a prowling bear.

¹⁶ A ruler without good sense will be a cruel tyrant. One who hates dishonesty will rule a long time.

¹⁷ A man guilty of murder is digging his own grave as fast as he can. Don't try to stop him.

¹⁸ Be honest and you will be safe. Be dishonest and you will fail.ʳ

¹⁹ A hard-working farmer has plenty to eat. People who waste time will always be poor.

²⁰ An honest man will lead a full, happy life. But if you are in a hurry to get rich, you are going to be punished.

²¹ Prejudice is wrong. But some judges will do wrong to get even the smallest bribe.

²² A selfish man is in such a hurry to get rich that he does not know when poverty is about to strike.

²³ Correct a man, and afterward he will appreciate it more than flattery.

²⁴ Anyone who thinks it isn't wrong to steal from his parents is no better than a common thief.

²⁵ Selfishness only causes trouble. You are much better off to trust the Lord.

²⁶ It is foolish to follow your own opinions. Be safe, and follow the teachings of wise men.

²⁷ Give to the poor and you will never be in need. Pretend that poverty does not exist, and many people will curse you.

²⁸ People stay in hiding when bad men come to power. But when they fall from power, righteous men will rule again.

ʳ fail; *Hebrew adds* in one.

29 If you get more stubborn every time you are corrected, one day you will be crushed, and never recover.

2 Show me a righteous ruler and I will show you a happy people. Show me a wicked ruler, and I will show you a miserable people.

3 If you appreciate wisdom, your father will be proud of you.

It is a foolish waste to spend money on prostitutes.

4 When the king is concerned with justice, the nation will be strong, but when he is only concerned with money, he will ruin his country.

5 Flatter your friends and you set a trap for yourself.

6 Evil men are trapped in their own sins, while honest men are happy and free.

7 A good man knows the rights of the poor, but wicked men cannot understand such things.

8 People with no regard for others can throw whole cities into turmoil. Wise men keep things calm.

9 When an intelligent man brings a lawsuit against a fool, the fool only laughs, and becomes loud and abusive.

10 Bloodthirsty men hate an honest man, but righteous men will protect* his life.

11 A stupid man expresses his anger openly, but a sensible man is patient and holds it back.

12 If a ruler pays attention to false information, all his officials will be liars.

13 A poor man and his oppressor have this in common— the Lord gave eyes to both of them.

14 If a king defends the rights of the poor, he will rule for a long time.

15 Correction and discipline are good for children. If a child has his own way, he will make his mother ashamed of him.

16 When evil men are in power, crime increases. But the righteous will live to see the downfall of such men.

17 Discipline your son, and you can always be proud of him. He will never give you reason to be ashamed.

18 A nation without God's guidance is a nation without order. Happy is the man who keeps God's law!

* protect; *Hebrew* seek.

¹⁹ You cannot correct a servant just by talking to him. He may understand you, but he will pay no attention.

²⁰ There is more hope for a stupid fool than for someone who speaks without thinking.

²¹ Give your servant everything he wants from childhood on, and some day he will take over everything you own.

²² People with quick tempers cause a lot of quarreling and trouble.

²³ Arrogance is a man's downfall, but a man who is humble will be respected.

²⁴ A thief's partner is his own worst enemy. He will be punished if he tells the truth in court, and God will curse him if he doesn't.

²⁵ It is dangerous to be concerned with what others think of you, but it is safe to trust the Lord.

²⁶ Everybody wants the good will of the ruler, but only from the Lord can you get justice.

²⁷ The righteous hate the wicked, and the wicked hate the righteous.

The Words of Agur

30   These are the solemn words of Agur, son of Jakeh:
     "God is not with me, God is not with me,
        and I am helpless.[*]
  ² I am more like an animal than a man;
        I do not have the sense a man should have.
  ³ I have never learned any wisdom,
        and I know nothing at all about God.
  ⁴ Who has ever mastered heavenly knowledge?
        Who has ever caught the wind in his hand?
        Or wrapped up water in a piece of cloth?
        Or established the ends of the earth?
     Who is he, if you know? Who is his son?

⁵ "God keeps every promise he makes. He is like a shield for all who seek his protection. ⁶ If you claim that he said something that he never said, he will reprimand you, and show that you are a liar."

More Proverbs

⁷ I ask you, God, to let me have two things before I die:
⁸ keep me from lying, and let me be neither rich nor poor.

[*] "God . . . helpless; *Hebrew unclear.*

So give me only as much food as I need. ⁹ If I have more, I might say that I do not need you. But if I am poor, I might steal, and bring disgrace on my God.

¹⁰ Never criticize a servant to his master. You will be cursed, and suffer for it.

¹¹ There are people who curse their fathers, and do not show their appreciation for their mothers.

¹² There are people who think they are pure, when they are as filthy as they can be.

¹³ There are people who think they are so good—oh, how good they think they are!

¹⁴ There are people who take cruel advantage of the poor and needy; that is the way they make their living.

¹⁵ A leech has two daughters, and both are named "Give me!"

There are four things that are never satisfied:
¹⁶ the world of the dead,ᵘ
    a woman without children,
        dry ground that needs rain,
           and a fire burning out of control.

¹⁷ A man who makes fun of his father or despises his mother in her old ageᵛ ought to be eaten by vultures, or have his eyes picked out by wild ravens.

¹⁸ There are four things that are too mysterious for me to understand:
¹⁹ an eagle flying in the sky,
    a snake moving on a rock,
        a ship finding its way over the sea,
           and a man and a woman falling in love.

²⁰ This is how an unfaithful wife acts: she commits adultery, takes a bath, and says, "But I haven't done anything wrong!"

²¹ There are four things that the earth itself cannot tolerate:
²² a slave who becomes a king,
    a fool who has all he wants to eat,
²³   a hateful woman who gets married,
        and a servant girl who takes the place of her mistress.

ᵘ WORLD OF THE DEAD: See 2.18.
ᵛ *One ancient translation* mother in her old age; *Hebrew* mother's obedience.

[24] There are four animals in the world that are small, but very, very clever:

[25] Ants: they are weak, but they store up their food in the summer.

[26] Rock rabbits: they are not strong either, but they make their homes among the rocks.

[27] Locusts: they have no king, but they move in formation.

[28] Lizards: you can hold one in your hand, but you can find them in palaces.

[29] There are four things that are impressive to watch as they walk:

[30] lions, strongest of all animals, and afraid of none;

[31]   goats, strutting roosters,
        and kings in front of their people.[w]

[32] If you have been foolish enough to be arrogant, and plan evil, stop and think! [33] Churn milk and you get butter. Hit someone's nose and it bleeds. Stir up anger and you get into trouble.

Advice to a King

31 These are the solemn words which King Lemuel's mother said to him:

[2] "You are my own dear son, the answer to my prayers. What shall I tell you? [3] Don't spend all your energy on sex, and all your money on women; they have destroyed kings. [4] Listen, Lemuel. Kings should not drink wine, or have a craving for alcohol. [5] When they drink, they forget the laws, and ignore the rights of people in need. [6] Alcohol is for men who are dying, who are in misery. [7] Let them drink, and forget how poor and unhappy they are.

[8] "Speak up for people who cannot speak for themselves. Protect the rights of all who are helpless. [9] Speak for them, and be a righteous judge. Protect the rights of the poor and needy."

The Perfect Wife

[10] How hard it is to find a perfect wife! She is worth far more than jewels!

[11] Her husband puts his confidence in her, and he will never be poor.

---

[w] *Verse 31 in Hebrew is unclear.*

¹² As long as she lives, she does him good, and never harm.

¹³ She keeps herself busy making wool and linen cloth.

¹⁴ She brings home food from out-of-the-way places, as merchant ships do.

¹⁵ She gets up before daylight to prepare food for her family and to tell her servant girls what to do.

¹⁶ She looks at land, and buys it for a vineyard with money she has earned.

¹⁷ She is a hard worker, strong and industrious.

¹⁸ She knows the value of everything she makes, and works late into the night.

¹⁹ She spins her own thread and weaves her own cloth.

²⁰ She is generous to the poor and needy.

²¹ She doesn't worry when it snows, because her family has warm clothing.

²² She makes bedspreads, and wears clothes of fine purple linen.

²³ Her husband is well known, one of the leading citizens.

²⁴ She makes clothes and belts and sells them to merchants.

²⁵ She is strong and respected, and not afraid of the future.

²⁶ She speaks with a gentle wisdom.

²⁷ She is always busy, and looks after her family's needs.

²⁸ Her children show their appreciation, and her husband praises her.

²⁹ He says, "Many women are good wives, but you are the best of them all."

³⁰ Charm is deceptive and beauty disappears, but a woman who fears the Lord should be praised.

³¹ Give her credit for all she does. She deserves the respect of everyone.

She keeps herself busy

ECCLESIASTES

Life Is Useless

1 These are the words of the Philosopher, David's son, who was king in Jerusalem.

2 It is useless, useless, said the Philosopher. Life is useless, all useless. 3 You spend your life working, laboring, and what do you have to show for it? 4 Generations come and generations go, but the world stays just the same. 5 The sun still rises, and it still goes down, going wearily back to where it must start all over again. 6 The wind blows south, the wind blows north—round and round and back again. 7 Every river flows into the sea, but the sea is not yet full. The water returns to where the rivers began, and starts all over again. 8 Everything leads to weariness—a weariness too great for words. Our eyes can never see enough to be satisfied; our ears can never hear enough. 9 What has happened before will happen again. What has been done before will be done again. There is nothing new in the whole world. 10 "Look," they say, "here is something new!" But no, it has all happened before, long before we were born. 11 No one remembers what has happened in the past, and no one in days to come will remember what happens between now and then.

The Philosopher's Experience

12 I, the Philosopher, have been king over Israel in Jerusalem. 13 I determined that I would examine and study all the things that are done in this world.

God has laid a miserable fate upon us. 14 I have seen everything done in this world, and I tell you, it is all useless. It is like chasing the wind. 15 You can't straighten out what is crooked; you can't count things that aren't there.

16 I told myself, "I have become a great man, far wiser than anyone who ruled Jerusalem before me. I know what wisdom and knowledge really are." 17 I had determined to learn the difference between knowledge and foolishness, wisdom and madness. But I found out that I might as well be chasing the wind. 18 The wiser you are, the more worries you have; the more you know, the more it hurts.

2 I decided to enjoy myself and find out what happiness is. But I found that this is useless, too. ² I discovered that laughter is stupid, that pleasure does you no good. ³ Driven on by my desire for wisdom, I decided to cheer myself up with wine and have a good time. Maybe, I thought, this is the best thing people can do during their short lives on earth.

⁴ I accomplished great things. I built myself houses and planted vineyards. ⁵ I planted gardens and orchards, with all kinds of fruit trees in them; ⁶ I dug ponds to irrigate them. ⁷ I bought many slaves, and there were slaves born in my household. I owned more livestock than anyone else who had ever lived in Jerusalem. ⁸ I also piled up silver and gold from the royal treasuries of the lands I ruled. Men and women sang to entertain me, and I had all the women a man could want.

⁹ Yes, I was great, greater than anyone else who had ever lived in Jerusalem, and my wisdom never failed me. ¹⁰ Anything I wanted, I got. I did not deny myself any pleasure. I was proud of everything I had worked for, and this was my reward. ¹¹ Then I thought about all that I had done, and how hard I had worked doing it, and I realized that it didn't mean a thing. It was like chasing the wind— of no use at all. ¹² After all, a king can only do what previous kings have done.

So I started thinking about what it meant to be wise, or reckless, or foolish. ¹³ Oh, I know, "Wisdom is better than foolishness, just as light is better than darkness. ¹⁴ Wise men can see where they are going, and fools cannot." But I also know that the same fate is waiting for us all. ¹⁵ I thought to myself, "What happens to fools is going to happen to me, too. So what have I gained from being so wise?" "Nothing," I answered, "not a thing." ¹⁶ No one remembers wise men, and no one remembers fools. In days to come, we will all be forgotten. We must all die— wise and foolish alike. ¹⁷ So life came to mean nothing to me, because everything in it had brought me nothing but trouble. It had all been useless; I had been chasing the wind.

¹⁸ Nothing that I had worked for and earned meant a thing to me, because I knew that I would have to leave it to my successor, ¹⁹ and he might be wise, or he might be

The best thing a man can do

foolish—who knows? Yet he will own everything I have worked for, everything my wisdom has earned for me in this world. It is all useless. ²⁰ So I came to regret that I had worked so hard. ²¹ You work for something with all your wisdom, knowledge, and skill, and then you have to leave it all to someone who hasn't had to work for it. It is useless, and it isn't right! ²² You work and worry your way through life, and what do you have to show for it? ²³ Everything you do, as long as you live, brings nothing but worry and heartache. Even at night your mind can't rest. It is all useless.

²⁴ The best thing a man can do is eat and drink, and enjoy what he has earned. And yet, I realized that even this comes from God. ²⁵ How else could you have anything to eat, or enjoy yourself at all? ²⁶ God gives wisdom, knowledge, and happiness to those he likes, but he makes others work, earning and saving, so that what they get can be given to someone he likes better. It is all useless. It is like chasing the wind.

A Time for Everything

3 Everything that happens in this world happens at the time God chooses.

> ² He sets the time for birth and the time for death;
> the time for planting and the time for pulling up;
> ³ the time for killing and the time for healing;
> the time for tearing down and the time for building.
> ⁴ He sets the time for sorrow and the time for joy;
> the time for mourning and the time for dancing;
> ⁵ the time for having sex and the time for not having it;
> the time for kissing and the time for not kissing.
> ⁶ He sets the time for finding and the time for losing;
> the time for saving and the time for throwing away;

⁷ the time for tearing and the time for mend-
ing;
the time for silence and the time for talk.
⁸ He sets the time for love and the time for
hate;
the time for war and the time for peace.

⁹ What does a man gain from all his work? ¹⁰ I know the
fate that God has laid on us. ¹¹ He has set the right time
for everything. He has given us a desire to know the
future, but never gives us the satisfaction of fully understanding what he does. ¹² So I realized that all a man can
do is be happy and do the best he can while he is still
alive. ¹³ All of us should eat and drink, and enjoy what
we have worked for. It is God's gift.

¹⁴ I know that everything God does will last forever.
You can't add anything to it or take anything away from
it. And one thing God does is to make men fear him.
¹⁵ Whatever happens or can happen has already happened
before. God makes the same thing happen again and again.

Injustice in the World

¹⁶ Not only this, I have also noticed that in this world
you find wickedness where justice and right ought to be.
¹⁷ I told myself, "God is going to judge the righteous and
the evil alike, because every thing, every action, will happen at its own set time."ᵃ ¹⁸ I decided that God is testing men,
to show them that they are no better than animals. ¹⁹ After
all, the same fate awaits men and animals alike. One dies
just like the other. They are the same kind of creature.
A man is no better off than an animal, because life has no
meaning for either. ²⁰ They are both going to the same
place—the dust. They both came from it; they will both
go back to it. ²¹ How can anyone be sure that a man's
spirit goes upward, while an animal's spirit goes down into
the ground? ²² So I realized then that the best thing a man
can do is enjoy what he has worked for. There is nothing
else he can do. There is no way for him to know what will
happen after he dies.

4 Then I looked again at all the injustice that goes on
in this world. The oppressed were crying, and no one
would help them. No one would help them, because their

ᵃ *Hebrew adds* there.

oppressors had power on their side. ² I envy those who are dead and gone; they are better off than those who are still alive. ³ But better off than either are those who have never been born, who have never seen the injustice that goes on in this world.

⁴ I have also learned why people work so hard to succeed: it is because they want to have more than anyone else. But it is useless. It is like chasing the wind. ⁵ They say that a man would be a fool to fold his hands and let himself starve to death. ⁶ Maybe so, but it is better to have only a little, with peace of mind, than be busy all the time with both hands, trying to catch the wind.

⁷ I have noticed something else in life that is useless. ⁸ Here is a man who lives alone. He has no son, no brother, yet he is always working, never satisfied with the wealth he has. For whom is he working so hard and denying himself any happiness? This is useless, too—and a miserable way to live.

⁹ Two are better off than one, because together they can work more effectively. ¹⁰ If one of them falls down, the other can help him up. But if someone is alone and falls, it's just too bad, because there is no one to help him. ¹¹ If it is cold, two can sleep together and stay warm, but how can you keep warm by yourself? ¹² Two men can resist an attack that would defeat one man alone. A rope made of three cords is hard to break.

¹³⁻¹⁴ A man may rise from poverty to become king of his country, or go from prison to the throne, but if in his old age he is too foolish to take advice, he is not as well off as a young man who is poor, but intelligent. ¹⁵ I thought about all the people who live in this world, and I realized that somewhere among them there is a young man who will take the king's place. ¹⁶ There may be no limit to the number of people a king rules; when he is gone, no one will be grateful for what he has done. It is useless. It is like chasing the wind.

Don't Make Rash Promises

5 Be careful about going to the temple. Go there to learn. That is better than to offer sacrifices like foolish people who don't know right from wrong. ² Think before you speak, and don't make any rash promises

to God. He is in heaven and you are on earth, so don't say any more than you have to. ³ The more you worry, the more likely you are to have bad dreams, and the more you talk, the more likely you are to say something foolish. ⁴ So when you make a promise to God, hurry and keep it. He has no use for a fool. Do what you promise to do. ⁵ Better not to promise at all than to make a promise and not keep it. ⁶ Don't let your own words lead you into sin, so that you have to tell God's priest that you didn't mean it. Why make God angry with you? Why let him destroy what you have worked for? ⁷ In spite of all your dreams, all your useless work and many words, you must still fear God.

Life Is Useless

⁸ Don't be surprised when you see that the government oppresses the poor, and denies them justice and their rights. Every official is protected by the one over him, and both are protected by still higher officials.

⁹ Even a king depends on the harvest.ᵇ

¹⁰ If you love money, you will never be satisfied; if you long to be rich, you will never get all you want. It is useless. ¹¹ The richer you are, the more mouths you have to feed. All you gain is the knowledge that you are rich. ¹² A working man may or may not have enough to eat, but at least he can get a good night's sleep. A rich man, though, has so much that he stays awake worrying.

¹³ Here is a terrible thing that I have seen in this world: people save up their money for a time when they may need it, ¹⁴ and then lose it all in some bad deal, so that they have nothing left to pass on to their children. ¹⁵ We leave this world just as we entered it—with nothing. In spite of all our work, there is nothing we can take with us. ¹⁶ It isn't right! We go just as we came. We labor, trying to catch the wind, and what do we get? ¹⁷ We get to live our lives in darkness and grief,ᶜ worried, angry, and sick.

¹⁸ Here is what I have found out: the best thing anyone can do is eat and drink, and enjoy what he has worked for during the short life that God has given him; this is man's fate. ¹⁹ If God gives a man wealth and property, and lets

ᵇ Verse 9 in Hebrew is unclear.
ᶜ Some ancient translations in darkness and grief; Hebrew eating in darkness.

him enjoy them, he should be grateful and enjoy what he has worked for. It is a gift from God. ²⁰ Since God has allowed him to be happy, he will not worry too much about how short life is.

6   I have noticed that in this world a serious injustice is done to man. ² God will give someone wealth, honor, and property, yes, everything he wants, but then will not let him enjoy it. Some stranger will enjoy it instead. It is useless, and it just isn't right. ³ A man may have a hundred children, and live a long time, but no matter how long he lives, if he does not get his share of happiness, and does not receive a decent burial, then I say that a baby born dead is better off. ⁴ It does that baby no good to be born; it disappears into darkness, where it is forgotten. ⁵ It never sees the light of day, or knows what life is like, but at least it has found rest—⁶ more so than the man who never enjoys life, though he may live two thousand years. After all, both of them are going to the same place.

⁷ A man does all his work just to get something to eat, but he never has enough. ⁸ How is a wise man better off than a fool? What good does it do a poor man to know how to face life? ⁹ It is useless; it is like chasing the wind. It is better to be satisfied with what you have than to be always wanting something else.

¹⁰ Everything that happens was already determined long ago, and we all know that a man cannot argue with what is stronger than he is. ¹¹ The longer you argue, the more useless it is, and you are no better off. ¹² How can anyone know what is best for a man in this short, useless life of his—a life that passes like a shadow? How can anyone know what will happen in the world after he dies?

Thoughts about Life

7   A good reputation is better than expensive perfume; and the day you die is better than the day you are born.

² It is better to go to a home where there is mourning than to one where there is a party, because the living should always remind themselves that death is waiting for us all.

³ Sorrow is better than laughter; it may sadden your face, but it sharpens your understanding.

It is useless; it is like chasing the wind

[4] A man who is always thinking about happiness is a fool. A wise man thinks about death.

[5] It is better to have a wise man reprimand you than to have stupid people sing your praises.

[6] When a fool laughs, it is like thorns crackling in a fire. It doesn't mean a thing.

[7] When a wise man cheats someone, he is acting like a fool. Take a bribe and you ruin your character.

[8] It is better when something ends than when it begins. Patience is better than pride.

[9] Keep your temper under control; it is foolish to harbor a grudge.

[10] Never ask, "Oh, why were things so much better in the old days?" It's not an intelligent question.

[11] Everyone who lives ought to be wise; it is as good as receiving an inheritance, [12] and will give you as much security as money can. Wisdom keeps you safe—this is the advantage of knowledge.

[13] Think about what God has done. How can anyone straighten out what God has made crooked? [14] When things are going well for you, be glad, and when trouble comes, just remember: God sends both happiness and trouble; you never know what is going to happen next.

[15] My life has been useless, but in it I have seen everything. A good man may die, while another man lives on, even though he is evil. [16] So don't be too good or too wise —why kill yourself? [17] But don't be too wicked or too foolish, either—why die before you have to? [18] Avoid both extremes. If you fear God you will be successful anyway.

[19] Wisdom does more for a man than ten rulers can do for a city.

[20] There is not a man on earth who does what is right all the time and never makes a mistake.

[21] Don't pay attention to everything people say—you may hear your servant insulting you, [22] and you know yourself that you have insulted other people many times.

[23] I used my wisdom to test all of this. I was determined to be wise, but it was beyond me. [24] How can anyone discover what life means? It is too deep for us, too hard to understand. [25] But I devoted myself to knowledge and study; I was determined to find wisdom and the answers

to my questions, and to learn how wicked and foolish stupidity is.

²⁶ I found something more bitter than death—a woman. The love she offers you will catch you like a trap, like a net; and her arms around you will hold you like a chain. A man who pleases God can get away, but she will catch the sinner. ²⁷ Yes, said the Philosopher, I found this out little by little, while I was looking for answers. ²⁸ I have looked for other answers but have found none. I found one man in a thousand that I could respect, but not one woman. ²⁹ This is all that I have learned: God made us plain and simple, but we have made ourselves very complicated.

8 Only a wise man knows what things really mean. Wisdom makes him smile, and makes his frowns disappear.

Obey the King

² Do what the king says,ᵈ and don't make any rash promises to God. ³ The king can do anything he likes, so leave his presence; don't stay in such a dangerous place. ⁴ The king acts with authority, and no one can challenge what he does. ⁵ As long as you obey his commands you are safe, and a wise man knows how and when to do it. ⁶ There is a right time and a right way to do everything, but we know so little! ⁷ None of us knows what is going to happen, and who is there to tell us? ⁸ No one can keep himself from dying, or put off the day of his death. That is a battle we cannot escape; we cannot cheat our way out.

The Wicked and the Righteous

⁹ I saw all this when I thought about the things that are done in this world, a world where some men have power, and others have to suffer under them. ¹⁰ Yes, I have seen wicked men buried and in their graves, but on the way back from the cemetery, people praise them in the very city where they did their evil.ᵉ It is useless.

¹¹ Why do people commit crimes so readily? Because crime is not punished quickly enough. ¹² A sinner may commit a hundred crimes and still live. Oh yes, I know what they say: "If you fear God everything will be all right, ¹³ but it will not go well for the wicked. Their life is

ᵈ *Some ancient translations* Do what the king says; *Hebrew unclear.*
ᵉ *Verse 10 in Hebrew is unclear.*

like a shadow, and they will die young, because they do not fear God." [14] But this is nonsense. Look at what happens in the world: sometimes righteous men get the punishment of the wicked and wicked men get the reward of the righteous. I say it is useless.

[15] So I am convinced that a man should enjoy himself, because the only pleasure he has in this life is eating and drinking, and enjoying himself. He can at least do this as he labors during the life that God has given him in this world.

[16] Whenever I tried to become wise, and learn what goes on in the world, I realized that you could stay awake night and day [17] and never be able to understand what God is doing. However hard you try, you will never find out. Wise men may claim to know, but they don't.

9 I thought long and hard about all this, and saw that God controls the actions of wise and righteous men, even their love and their hate. No one knows anything about what lies ahead of him. [2] It makes no difference. The same fate comes to the righteous and the wicked, to the good and the bad,[f] to those who are religious and those who are not, to those who worship and those who do not. A good man is no better off than a sinner; a man who takes an oath is no better off than one who does not. [3] One fate comes to all alike, and this is as wrong as anything that happens in this world. As long as people live, their minds are full of evil and madness, and suddenly they die. [4] But anyone who is alive, in the world of the living, has some hope; better a live dog than a dead lion. [5] Yes, the living know they are going to die, but the dead know nothing. They have no further reward; they are completely forgotten. [6] Their loves, their hates, their passions all died with them. They will never again take part in anything that happens in this world.

[7] Go ahead—eat your food and be happy; drink your wine and be cheerful. It's all right with God. [8] Always look happy and cheerful. [9] Enjoy life with the woman you love, as long as you live the useless life that God has given you in this world. Enjoy every useless day of it, because that is all you will get for your trouble. [10] Work hard at whatever you do, because there will be no action, no

f *Some ancient translations* and the bad; *Hebrew omits.*

thought, no knowledge, no wisdom in the land of the dead*
—and that is where you are going.

¹¹ I realized another thing, that in this world fast runners
do not always win the races, and the brave do not always
win the battles. Wise men do not always earn a living,
intelligent men do not always get rich, and capable men do
not always rise to high positions. Bad luck happens to
everyone. ¹² You never know when your time is coming.
Like birds suddenly caught in a trap, like fish caught in a
net, we are trapped at some evil moment when we least
expect it.

Thoughts on Wisdom and Foolishness

¹³ There is something else I saw, a good example of how
wisdom is regarded in this world. ¹⁴ There was a little
town, without many people in it. A powerful king attacked
it. He surrounded it and prepared to break through the
walls. ¹⁵ There was a man there who was poor, but so
clever that he could have saved the town. But no one
thought about him. ¹⁶ I have always said that wisdom is
better than strength, but no one thinks of a poor man as
wise, or pays any attention to what he says. ¹⁷ It is better
to listen to the quiet words of a wise man than to the
shouts of a ruler at a council of fools. ¹⁸ Wisdom does
more good than weapons, but one mistake can undo a
lot of good.

10 Dead flies can make a whole jar of perfume stink,
and a little stupidity can cancel out the greatest
wisdom.

² It is natural for a wise man to do the right thing, and
for a fool to do the wrong thing. ³ His stupidity will be
evident even to strangers; he lets everyone know that he
is a fool.

⁴ If your ruler becomes angry with you, do not hand in
your resignation; serious wrongs may be pardoned if you
keep calm.

⁵ Here is an injustice I have seen in the world—an injustice caused by rulers. ⁶ Stupid people are given positions
of authority, while rich men are ignored. ⁷ I have seen
slaves on horseback while noblemen walk like slaves.

---

g LAND OF THE DEAD: It was thought that the dead continued to exist in a dark
world under the ground.

We are trapped at some evil moment

⁸ Dig a pit and you fall in it; break through a wall and a snake bites you. ⁹ Dig for stone and you get hurt by stones. Split wood and you get hurt doing it. ¹⁰ If your ax is dull and you don't sharpen it, you have to work harder to use it. It is smarter to plan ahead. ¹¹ Knowing how to charm a snake is of no use if you let the snake bite first. ¹² What a wise man says brings him honor, but a fool is destroyed by his own words. ¹³ He starts out with silly talk, and ends up with pure madness. ¹⁴ A fool talks on and on.

No one knows what is going to happen next, and no one can tell us what will happen after we die.

¹⁵ Only a man too stupid to find his way home would wear himself out working.

¹⁶ A country is in trouble when its king is easily influenced, and its leaders feast all night long. ¹⁷ But a country is fortunate to have a king who makes his own decisions, and leaders who eat at the proper time, who control themselves and don't get drunk.

¹⁸ When a man is too lazy to repair his roof, it will leak, and the house will fall in.

¹⁹ Feasting makes you happy and wine cheers you up, but you can't have either without money.

²⁰ Don't criticize the king, even silently, and don't criticize the rich, even in the privacy of your bedroom. A bird might carry the message and tell them what you said.

What a Wise Man Does

11 Invest your money in foreign trade, and one of these days you will make a profit. ² Put your investments in several places—many places even—because you never know what kind of bad luck you are going to have in this world.

³ No matter which direction a tree falls, it will lie where it fell. When the clouds are full, it rains. ⁴ If you wait until the wind and the weather are just right, you will never plant anything, and never harvest anything. ⁵ God made everything, and you can no more understand what he does than you understand how new life begins in the womb of a pregnant woman. ⁶ Do your planting in the morning and in the evening, too. You never know whether it will all grow well, or whether one planting will do better than the other.

⁷ It is good to be able to enjoy the pleasant light of day.
⁸ Be grateful for every year you live. No matter how long
you live, remember that you will be dead much longer.
There is nothing at all to look forward to.

Advice to Young People

⁹ Young people, enjoy your youth. Be happy while you
are still young. Do what you want to do, and follow your
heart's desire. (But remember that God is going to judge
you for whatever you do.)
¹⁰ Don't let anything worry you or cause you pain. You
aren't going to be young very long.

12 So remember your Creatorʰ while you are still
young, before those dismal days and years come
when you will say, "I don't enjoy life." ² That is when the
light of the sun, the moon, and the stars will grow dim for
you, and the rain clouds will never pass away. ³ Then your
arms, that have protected you, will tremble, and your legs,
now strong, will grow weak. Your teeth will be too few to
chew your food, and your eyes too dim to see clearly.
⁴ Your ears will be deaf to the noise of the street. You will
barely be able to hear the mill as it grinds, or music as it
plays, but even the song of a bird will wake you from
sleep. ⁵ You will be afraid of high places, and walking will
be dangerous. Your hair will turn white; your sexual vigor
will vanish and nothing can bring it back.

We are going to our final resting place, and then there will
be mourning in the streets. ⁶ The silver chain will snap,
and the golden lamp will fall and break; the rope at the well
will break, and the water jar will be shattered. ⁷ Our bodies
will return to the dust of the earth, and the breath of life
go back to God, who gave it to us.

⁸ Useless, useless, said the Philosopher. It is all useless.

The Summing Up

⁹ But because the Philosopher was wise, he kept on
teaching the people what he knew. He studied proverbs
and honestly tested their truth. ¹⁰ The Philosopher tried to
find comforting words, but the words he wrote were honest.
¹¹ The sayings of wise men are like the sharp sticks that

ʰ *The Hebrew word for* Creator *sounds like a Hebrew word for* grave.

There will be mourning in the streets

shepherds use to guide sheep.[i] They have been given by God, the one Shepherd of us all.

¹² Son, there is something else to watch out for. There is no end to the writing of books, and too much study will wear you out.

¹³ After all this, there is only one thing to say: Fear God, and obey his commands, because this is all that man was created for. ¹⁴ God is going to judge everything we do, whether good or bad, even things done in secret.

---

[i] like the . . . sheep; *Hebrew unclear.*

NOTES

NOTES

NOTES

NOTES

DATE DUE